Dedicated to Dan Mcdonald, who brought me to raw veganism and to Dr. Robert Morse, who taught me about deep tissue detoxification.

INDEX

Down To Earth Raw Vegan Recipes

Eating Healthy is simple!

VictoriaRawVegan

HEALING THROUGH RAW FOODS & DETOXIFICATION

CHECK ME OUT ON YOUTUBE!

About Victoria

I became enthralled with living foods in 2012 after seeing many YouTube videos telling the wonders and testimonies of raw veganism. I went raw overnight and I have not looked back since. I have healed my chronic cystic acne that plagued me for over ten years and skin problems that I have had since birth. My digestion and chronic bowel problems have been erased. My energy is through the roof and I only have detoxification to thank for these wonders. Raw food & healthy living have changed my life completely for the better and I am forever thankful.

Always choose organic produce!

VictoriaRawVegan

Always eat truly ripe produce!

RAW VEGAN BASICS

Eat lots of

FRUIT & GREENS

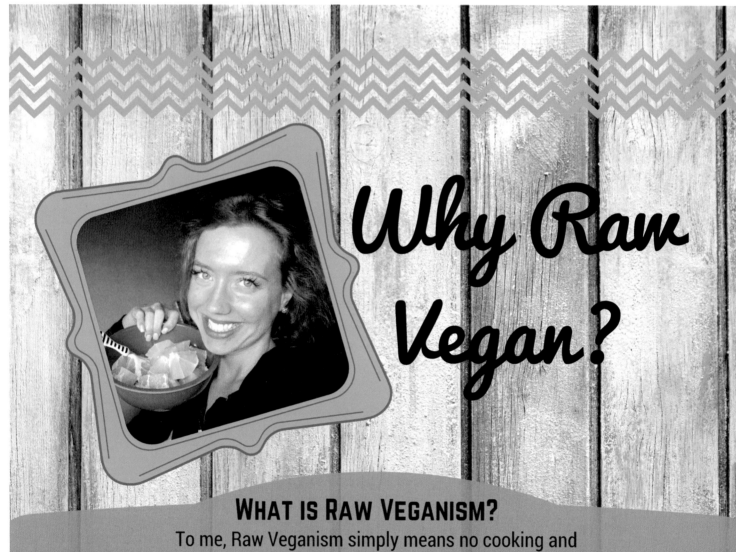

Why Raw Vegan?

WHAT IS RAW VEGANISM?

To me, Raw Veganism simply means no cooking and
only eating foods that are living and vibrant in their natural state.
I focus on mostly organic fruits with the inclusion
of lots of tender leafy greens and a modest amount
of soaked and sprouted nuts and seeds.
Raw Veganism encapsulates what I want most: vibrancy, peace to animals, &
loving the natural God-given foods everyday.
It's easy to be raw and the food tastes great, but most of all your body & its
health will become your best ally.
Detoxification comes as a natural part of Raw Veganism, which is essential to
long-term health. Getting rid of what is no longer wanted in the body while
strengthening the glands and organs synergistically is just what a high fruit raw
vegan diet will give you!

INCORPORATE

RAW JUICES

ALKALINE WATER

SUNLIGHT

FRESH AIR

Fully Encompass A Healthy Lifestyle!

sundried tomato DIP

1

Sundried Tomato Dip

In a food processor, blend all ingredients until you get a creamy consistency.
It should look like a hummus-type dish!
Enjoy!

- 2 heaping tablespoons raw organic tahini
- 2-3 small zucchinis
- 1 package oil/salt free sun dried tomatoes
- Juice from 1 lemon
- 1 heaping tablespoon organic ground cumin

Vanilla Ice Cream
With Strawberries!

Vanilla Bean Ice Cream

WITH STRAWBERRIES!

In a high speed blender, blend as many frozen bananas as you desire with enough raw coconut water to make a thick ice cream. If you like it thicker or thinner, use more or less coconut water. Add 2 heaping tablespoons of raw vanilla bean powder.

Blend until you have ice cream!

Add chopped strawberries on top for an added treat!

Frozen bananas
(I use around 5 when I make this recipe)
2 heaping tablespoons
raw vanilla bean powder
Around 1-2 cups raw coconut water

STRAWBERRY ♥ ICE CREAM

Modify by using

any fruit

you fancy!

3

Strawberry Ice Cream

In a high speed blender, blend as many frozen bananas as you desire with enough raw coconut water to make a thick ice cream. If you like it thicker or thinner, use more or less coconut water.

Add one bag of frozen strawberries or one carton of fresh strawberries!

Blend until you have ice cream!

Frozen bananas (I use around 5 when I make this recipe)
1 bag of frozen strawberries or
1 carton of fresh strawberries
Around 1-2 cups raw coconut water

BANANA ④
CINNAMON ROLLS

Banana Cinnamon Rolls

Chop around 5-10 bananas vertically in very thin slices.
Take the slices and place on a sheet in the dehydrator.
Sprinkle cinnamon on top of the slices.
Dehydrate for 9 hours on 110 degrees.
When they are done, carefully coil the slices into the shape of cinnamon rolls.
Sauce:
In a high speed blender add: around 15 dates, 5 dashes of cinnamon, a few splashes of raw coconut water, 2 tbsp raw carob powder (optional) &/or 2 tbsp raw vanilla bean powder (optional).

5-10 ripe bannas
Around 15 dates
Cinnamon
Raw coconut water
Raw carob powder (optional)
Raw vanilla bean powder (optional)

NORI
JICAMA
SALAD

Nori Jicama Salad

In a food processor, shred 1 large jicama
and 1 large carrot.
Place into a large bowl and add chopped celery,
red and yellow bell pepper, cucumber,
and any other vegetables you like!
Then rip up 2 raw nori sheets into
small pieces and add to the bowl.
Mix well.
Dressing:
*Use the basic tahini dressing (Recipe 19)

1 large jicama
1 large carrot
2 raw nori sheets
Red and yellow bell peppers
Celery
Cucumber

RAINBOW SUSHI

6

Rainbow Sushi

In a food processor, shred 4 carrots, 1 beet, and 1 zucchini. Place in bowl. Slice thinly celery, cucumber, and avocado.
Spread the shredded mixture onto nori sheets and add the sliced ingredients.
Roll into a burrito and slice into sushi rolls.
Enjoy!

4 carrots
1 beet
1 zucchini
2 stalks celery
1/2 of 1 cucumber
1/2 avocado
Raw nori sheets

CARROT CAKE COOKIES

7

Carrot Cake Cookies

In a food processor, shred enough carrots to make around 3 cups of shredded carrots. Replace the shredder attachment with the S-blade and blend the carrots, one small thumb of fresh ginger, around 5 dashes of cinnamon, 2 handfuls of raw pecans, and around 15-20 dates. Now take a handful of the mixture and make into whatever shape you'd like.
I used a heart shape cookie cutter, but you could make them into circles, balls, or any shape you want!

Carrots
Thumb of ginger
Cinnamon
2 handfuls raw pecans
Around 15-20 dates

8

RAW
VEGAN
SUSHI

Raw Vegan Sushi

In a food processor, shred enough carrots and jicama to
make around 4 cups.
Set aside.
Chop up celery, cucumber, and avocado in as thin slices
as possible.
Add any other ingredients you fancy!
Take a raw nori sheet and place the jicama and carrot
mixture, and a few slices of each ingredient and roll into
a large burrito.
Slice very carefully into sushi rolls.
Enjoy!

1 large jicama
2 carrots
Cucumber
Celery
1 avocado
Raw nori sheets

9

CREAMY TAHINI SALAD

Using the Basic Tahini Dressing!

Creamy Tahini Salad

Cut around 2 heads of romaine lettuce into thin strips.
Chop up any vegetables you like!
I used red peppers, celery, carrots, and cucumber.
Mix up the Basic Tahini Dressing (Recipe 19)
and stir it into the salad.
Enjoy!

2 heads romaine lettuce
Red pepper
Carrots
Cucumber
Celery
+ Ingredients for Basic Tahini Dressing

RAW VEGAN "BURGERS"

Delicious & Cruelty Free

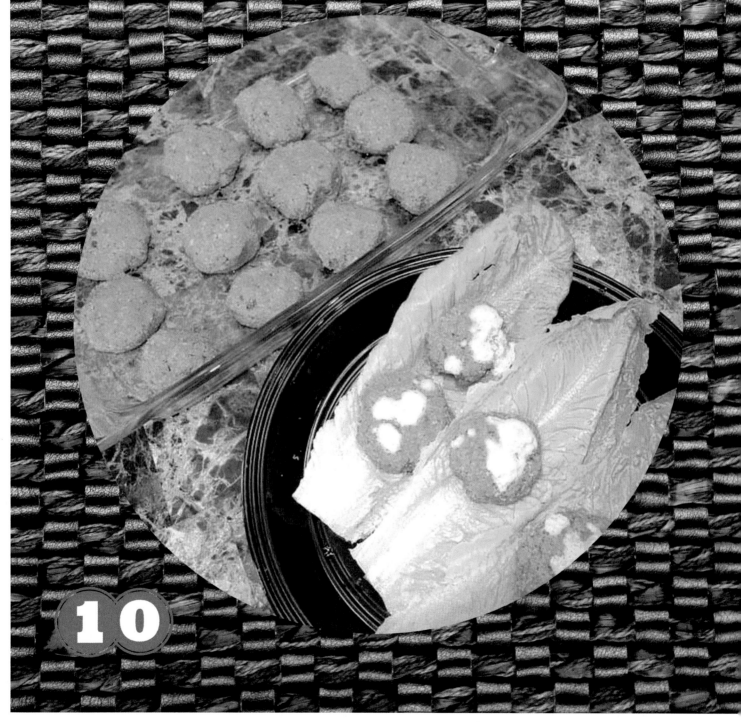

10

Raw Vegan Burgers

In a food processor, blend about 8 chopped carrots, 1 cup soaked sunflower seeds, 5 sundried tomatoes, several dashes of garlic & herb seasoning, and a few dashes of cayenne. Blend well.
Form into patties or balls.
Place them on top of romaine lettuce and top with Basic Tahini Dressing (Recipe 19) and tomatoes!

8 carrots
1 cup soaked sunflower seeds
5 sundried tomatoes (oil free)
Garlic & Herb seasoning
Cayenne
3 sliced tomatoes (for on top)

11

Apples & Caramel Dipping Sauce!

Always use fresh organic dates!

Apples & Caramel Dipping Sauce

In a high speed blender, add around 15 dates, 5 or more dashes of cinnamon, and enough raw coconut water to make a creamy consistency.
If you like a thicker sauce use less coconut water and vice versa.
Chop up apples to dip and you're done!
Enjoy!

15 dates
Raw coconut water
Cinnamon
Apples

Mango Chutney Salad!

12

Mango Chutney Salad

In a food processor, add 1 mango, 2 small zucchinis, a few dashes of cayenne, and 1 tbsp apple cider vinegar.
Pulse and blend until you get a chunky consistency.
Place onto a bed of chopped greens and add chopped cucumber and red onion on top.

1 mango
2 small zucchinis
1 tbsp ACV
Cayenne

HERB ICE

ADD TO WATER FOR A WONDERFUL TREAT!

Herb Ice

Chop up lemons, strawberries, and mint leaves.
Put water of your choice (I enjoy alkaline spring
water from glass bottles) into ice trays.
Add the chopped ingredients.
Freeze overnight.
Add to water for a refreshing, hydrating, and
mineralizing treat!
Enjoy!

Strawberries
Lemons
Mint leaves

BANANA ICE CREAM & DATES!

Banana Ice Cream & Dates

In a high speed blender, add around 5 frozen bananas and enough raw coconut water to make an ice cream consistency.
This can be trial and error depending on how many bananas you use.
The more liquid you use the easier it will be to blend.
Place into bowl and add chopped dates (around 8 or so).
Enjoy!

5 frozen bananas
8 dates (approx.)
Raw coconut water

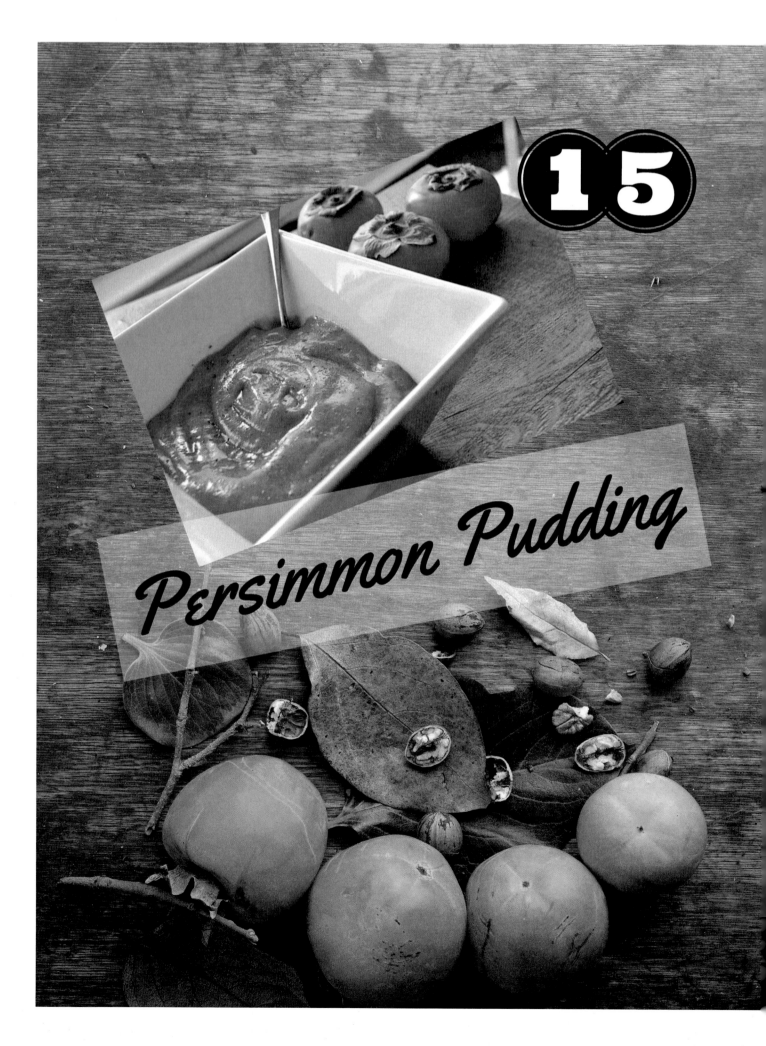

15

Persimmon Pudding

Persimmon Pudding

In a high speed blender, add around 5
truly ripe persimmons, around 10 dates,
a few dashes of cinnamon, and a
quarter of a sugar pumpkin.
Blend until creamy.
Enjoy this seasonal sweet treat!

5 persimmons
10 dates
Cinnamon
1/4 sugar pumpkin

Coleslaw!

Coleslaw

In a food processor, shred 3 medium
zucchinis and 5 carrots.
Place in large bowl.
Add 1 chopped english cucumber, 2 tbsp soaked
pumpkin seeds, 2 tbsp raw tahini, and several
dashes of mustard seed and paprika.
Add 5 dashes of cayenne and 6 tbsp ACV.
Mix well.
Place onto romaine leaves.
Enjoy!

3 medium zucchinis
5 carrots
1 english cucumber
2 tbsp soaked
pumpkin seeds
2 tbsp raw tahini
Mustard seed
Paprika
Cayenne
ACV

Mango Red Pepper Dressing!

17

Mango Red Pepper Dressing

In a blender, put 1-2 mangos, 1 red pepper, a few dashes of cayenne, and 4 tbsp apple cider vinegar.
Blend.
Pour over lettuce or dip lettuce into it like a dip!

1-2 mangos
4 tbsp ACV
Cayenne
1 red pepper

VANILLA BEAN ICECREAM

With Raw Mulberries!

18

Vanilla Bean Ice Cream with Mulberries

In a blender, add around 5 frozen bananas, 3 tbsp raw vanilla bean powder, and enough raw coconut water to make an ice cream consistency.
Blend well.
Add raw mulberries on top!
Enjoy!

5 frozen bananas
3 tbsp raw vanilla bean powder
Raw coconut water

Basic Tahini Dressing

19

Basic Tahini Dressing

This dressing is delicious and it is my go-to for an easy salad!

In a small bowl place two tbsp raw tahini, 1 tbsp chia seeds, the juice of 1 lemon, a few dashes of cayenne, and around 4 tbsp apple cider vinegar.

Stir thoroughly.

The dressing will thicken after a few minutes.

Enjoy!

1 lemon

2 tbsp raw tahini

Cayenne

1 tbsp chia seeds

Apple cider vinegar

"CHOCOLATE" COVERED STRAWBERRIES

21

"Chocolate" Covered Strawberries

In a blender, add around 15-20 dates, 3 tbsp raw carob powder, several dashes of cinnamon, and 1 cup of raw coconut water.
Blend well.
Take each strawberry and dip it in the chocolate sauce.

Around 2 cartons strawberries
15-20 dates
Raw coconut water
Cinnamon
3 tbsp raw carob powder

easy

RAW

SANDWICHES

20

Easy Raw Sandwiches

On a romaine lettuce leaf, add raw tahini, tomato, avocado, cucumber, and any vegetables you like.
Sprouts would be great on this!
Add Bragg's Sprinkles seasoning or any seasoing you like for added flavor.

Romaine lettuce
Avocado
Cucumber
Tomato
Seasonings of your choice

CHILI

22

Chili

In a food processor, blend tomatoes,
dates, sundried tomatoes, and spices.
Pour mixture on top of corn
in a large bowl.
Chop up the bell peppers and half of 1
tomato and mix into the bowl.
Enjoy with lots of greens!

3-4 medium beefsteak tomatoes
2 dates
Organic non-GMO corn (fresh is best)
One package sundried tomatoes
(oil/salt free preferably)
Quarter of orange and red bell pepper
1 tbsp cumin
Cayenne

CORN SALSA! 23

Corn Salsa

Chop up all of the ingredients and place
on top of corn in a large bowl.
Mix well.
Add spices and lime juice .
You're done!
This corn salsa is great mixed into
chopped greens.

5 roma tomatoes
1/2 red onion
Juice of 3 limes
1 handful chopped cilantro
Couple dashes cayenne
1/2 large jalapeno (take out the seeds/membranes)
1 bag frozen organic non-GMO corn
1/4 red bell pepper

VictoriaRawVegan

Creamy
Tomato
Dressing

Creamy Tomato Dressing

In a food processor, place the tomatoes, tahini, apple cider vinegar, zucchini (optional) and a few dashes of cayenne.
Blend until creamy.
This dresing is great on top of chopped romaine lettuce!

2 roma tomatoes
2 tbsp raw tahini
2 tbsp ACV
Cayenne
2 small zucchinis (optional-
this just adds more volume)

STACKED SALAD

STACK IT UP!

25

Stacked Salad

In a bowl (a round see through bowl is fun!) add all chopped ingredients in layers. I like doing the lettuce at the bottom and adding other ingredients on top.

Lettuce of your choice
Purple cabbage
Celery
Carrots
+ any veggies you want!

26

CABBAGE SLAW *Tacos*

Cabbage Slaw Tacos

In a food processor, shred the carrots and cabbage and place in a large bowl. The rest of the ingredients create the sauce. Blend all of them in the food processor.
Stir in the sauce into the shredded mixture.
Take the slaw and place inside of romaine lettuce.
You're done!

1/2 head green and purple cabbage
2 large carrots
2 large zucchinis
1 stalk celery
2 or 3 dates
2 tbsp raw tahini
2 tbsp raw hemp seeds
1/2 tsp turmeric
1/2 tsp cayenne

Cherry Cookies

These are
a
must-try!

27

Cherry Cookies

In a food processor, blend the dates, 1 cup of raw coconut water, and several dashes of cinnamon.

Form into any cookie shape you want. Defrost a bag of frozen cherries and place on top of the cookies (or use fresh cherries!)

Around 20 dates

1 cup raw coconut water

Cinnamon

Organic frozen cherries

Veggie Pizza! 28

Veggie Pizza

In a food processor, blend the pizza crust ingredients.
Place in a dehydrator for 12 hours on 105 degrees
in a large pizza shape.
When it's done dehydrating, spread the pizza sauce on top.
Add any toppings you like!
I used zucchini, carrots, and spinach!

Pizza Crust:

6 tbsp soaked raw
sunflower seeds
4 tbsp raw hemp seeds
Handful organic spinach
1 small carrot
1/2 cherry pepper (or a
few dashes of cayenne)
Dash of dried oregano
& basil
1/4 red onion
(or green onions)

Pizza Sauce:

Blend 2 roma
tomatoes, a couple
cherry peppers or a
few dashes of
cayenne, as many
sundried tomatoes as
you like, and several
dashes of dried basil
and oregano in the
food processor until
creamy.

Chunky Mango Chutney

29

Chunky Mango Chutney

In a food processor, pulse and blend
the mango, zucchini, raw tahini,
ACV, and cayenne.
You will want a chunky consistency.
Spread onto the lettuce of your choice
or use as a dip as shown
with carrots, lettuce or celery.

2 small zucchinis
3-4 mangoes
2 tbsp raw tahini
Couple dashes cayenne
3-4 tbsp apple cider vinegar

Dandelion Beet Juice!

Dandelion Beet Juice

In a masticating juicer, juice 1 bunch of dandelion (or less if you want it to be less pungent), 4 apples, and 1 large beet.
Enjoy this detoxifying treat!

1 bunch dandelion greens
4 apples
1 large beet

31

Creamy Pasta!

Creamy Pasta

In a large bowl, place your spiralized
zucchini inside and set aside.
In a smaller bowl, add the tahini, ACV,
lemon juice, and seasonings.
Blend with a fork until thoroughly mixed.
Blend into the zucchini noodles. Add
chopped red bell pepper (optional).
Enjoy!

2 tbsp raw tahini
3 tbsp apple cider vinegar
Juice of 1 lemon
1 tbsp dried basil and oregano
Couple dashes paprika and
cayenne
1 large zucchini
1/4 red bell epper

Creamy Corn
SALAD DRESSING

32

Creamy Corn Salad Dressing

In a blender, blend the corn, sundried
tomatoes, spices, ACV, lime juice
and green onions.
It's as simple as that!
Pour on top of a mound of greens!

6 fresh corns or 1 bag frozen
non-GMO organic corn
4 sundried tomatoes
Juice of 1 lime
3 green onions
2-3 tbsp garlic & herb seasoning
Couple dashes cayenne
4 tbsp apple cider vinegar

CHECK OUT
VICTORIARAWVEGAN.COM

"VictoriasRawDesigns"
on Etsy!